CONFIDENCE

Category: Business & Economics

2017 by Bob Oros Publishing

Standard Copyright License

ISBN 978-1-105-22694-6

Author: Bob Oros

Description: Remove restrictions and limitations. Your confidence will skyrocket when you learn how to remove the self imposed restrictions and limitations that hold people back from accomplishing all they can. Your goal will be to become a highly skilled sales professional. You will discover how to make a total commitment and it will be reflected in every action you take and every task you perform.

Key words: confidence, increase confidence,

SALTY DOG SYNDROME	4
YOUR ONE BIG THING	7
THE BIGGEST LOSER	10
HOW TO HANDLE REJECTION	15
A CONFIDENT SALES TEAM	25
SET THE STAGE	30
WHICH STATEMENTS ARE TRUE?	36
CONFIDENCE: REMOVE RESTRICTIONS AND LIMITATIONS	40
MY 4% IMPROVEMENT OBJECTIVE:	42
WHAT THE ENTIRE COURSE WILL DO FOR YOU	44
BEN FRANKLIN'S SYSTEM	45
ACHIEVE A 52% IMPROVEMENT	49
ABOUT THE AUTHOR BOB OROS (BOBOROS.COM),	51

Confidence
Remove restrictions and limitations

Salty dog syndrome

There were about 45 sales people in the meeting and I was presenting them with one of my products, a hot dog. It was not a new product but it was new to them. After everyone was just about finished sampling the hot dog everyone seemed sold on the product. Then, all of a sudden, someone said, "Man, these hot dogs are really salty!" Pretty soon everyone agreed they were salty. I knew the salty hot dogs would never sell so I had to act fast.

I told them that I would arrange to have the hot dogs picked up from their warehouse and send them another order that would be reformulated with less salt. Two weeks later I was again at the sales meeting presenting the same sales people with the reformulated hot dogs. Everyone agreed that they were much better. The formula with slightly less salt was a big improvement.

We had a great introduction offer for their customers and we sold tons of hot dogs. Everyone appreciated the extra effort I went to in order to give them the hot dog that they really wanted.

Here's the problem. I had the hot dogs picked up, put back in my warehouse, and two weeks later shipped the EXACT SAME HOT DOGS BACK TO THEM! Do you really think a company that was making millions of pounds of hot dogs every day with hundreds of thousands of customers all over the world who were very happy with the product would change the formula because one guy in a sales meeting said they were salty?

No way. And besides, they were not salty, they tasted great. But I had to make them think that I was able to have the hot dog reformulated. One guy out of the 45 sales people made an unthinking, uneducated comment, and pretty soon, the other 44 "sheep" believed him and started complaining about the salt content!

Now I have a really tough question for you. Are you one of the "sheep" who listens to someone on CNN and let them tell you that business is down, that no one is buying, that the hot dogs are salty? Are you one of the sheep who believe that politicians can create a cure-all for the economy? Are you one of the sheep who let other people tell you what and how to think while they knock your product and destroy your confidence? Or are you a confident enough sales person who has the guts to stand up and go into psychological warfare with yourself and your customers and be part of the solution rather than part of the problem?

If you stick with any prediction long enough, it will happen. The media is unrelenting in its attempt to manufacture an actual recession, or at least convince people there is one. If you hear it from CNN, FOX and MSNBC every single day, you will believe it. It is up to you to contradict the loud voices of gloom and doom telling your customers to lock up their money in fear. Money moves around, changes hands and gravitates to the person with an attitude for attracting it.

I didn't think the hot dogs were salty. I thought they tasted great. I wasn't about to let ONE uneducated sales person spoil my business!

Your ONE BIG THING

Years ago there was an essay written about the different types of government. The title of the essay was "The Fox Knew Many Things, But the Hedgehog Knew One Big Thing."

I never read the essay, but the title has a real good message for us in sales.

We all have some fox in us and know a lot of things, but to be successful in today's competitive market and really build your level of confidence you have to know ONE BIG THING.

It's easy to get side tracked and become like the fox, who knows all types of things, but here's the problem with knowing all types of things, you will not be KNOWN for anything. To have total confidence with your customers your ONE BIG THING has to be crystal clear in their mind as well as yours. You have to be looked upon as an expert.

If I am buying insurance I want to buy from a confident person whose ONE BIG THING is insurance. I want to deal with someone who "wrote the book" on insurance.

If I am buying or selling a house I want to deal with a confident person whose ONE BIG THING is real estate, NOT someone who is a dental assistant "thinking of getting into real estate on the side!"

Once you decide that selling is your ONE BIG THING you will be happier, healthier and more content with yourself. You will have a higher level of confidence and your self esteem will be as solid as a rock.

What keeps you from making the "do-or-die" decision that will give you that solid feeling that you are in control? There are a lot of ups and downs in selling, and when you have a down day you are at your weakest point. That is when you start to wonder why you have taken on such a difficult occupation. On the other hand, when you have a good day, you wouldn't trade it for anything.

If you look closely at a sail boat tacking into the wind it looks like it's going back and forth without getting anywhere. If you look at it from a distance, it's easy to see it is heading in a specific direction.

Selling is the same thing. If you look too closely at every presentation, every phone call, every turn-down, it will seem like you are getting nowhere. If you look at the week, month and quarter, you will see that you are making progress toward your goal.

To have the total respect of your customers you have to be committed to being a professional. You have to be a fanatic about your ONE BIG THING. If you spent just 30 minutes a day studying your products and your profession you would eventually be in the top 10% of your industry.

If I am buying a car I want the sales person's ONE BIG THING to be knowledge of the car. If I ask how wide the car's wheel base is I want them to know without him or her having to look it up.

If I own a restaurant I want to buy from someone whose ONE BIG THING is selling food and who has a passion for the restaurant business. Someone who can identify with me and "knows where I am coming from."

The biggest reason most sales people fail is because they never decide that SELLING is their one big thing. They never make the do-or-die decision that THIS IS IT. Once you make that decision, and stop thinking about what else you could be doing, your sales will take off.

The biggest loser

Let me ask you a question. Is selling an art or a science? What do you think?

If you said it is a science, you would be wrong. That doesn't mean you can't use scientific principles for your selling activities. It means selling itself cannot be a science. If you are trying to use scientific principles to predict your future sales plan you will have a hard time.

Here's why. In science every time you perform a certain act you will get the same result. Let's take boiling water. If you are at 5,000 feet above sea level water will boil at 203 degrees F. It will do it every time. You will always get the exact same outcome. If you boil water at 10,000 feet above sea level it will boil at 194 degrees F. It won't boil at 190 degrees or 193 degrees. It will boil only when the temperature reaches 194 degrees. Every time!

Here is a scientific chart that will make you feel certain about your knowledge. It has been tested and proven over and over again. There is no room for error. You can count on these numbers.

Sea Level	212 degrees F
984 ft.	210 degrees F
2,000 ft.	208 degrees F
3,000 ft.	206 degrees F
5,000 ft.	203 degrees F
7,500 ft.	198 degrees F

10,000 ft.   194 degrees F
20,000 ft.   178 degrees F
26,000 ft.   168 degrees F

Stay with me for a minute. I will show you why some people have such a difficult time in sales. I am not saying that only certain people can sell. I am saying that certain people have a harder time with the sales process than others. The reason is because they are more of a scientist than an artist. This is important to know when it comes to hiring and training as well as why you get so discouraged at times.

Selling is not a science, it is an art. In art every time you perform a certain act you get a variety of outcomes. An actor would be considered an artist. Ask 10 people what they thought of the actor in a play and you will get 10 different answers. This would be very difficult for a scientist because they would want the same predictable outcome from everyone who watched the play.

An artist can live with the fact that every time they do something they get a different outcome. A scientist has a more difficult time because they want a predictable outcome for every action.

A sales person has to deal with people and you and I both know that people are not predictable. We are under continuous influence by thousands of things everyday. Any one of these things can make us change our minds about something.

If sales could be reduced to a science we would not need any sales people. We would only need order takers, or a system to get the order turned in.

If selling was a science, what fun would it be? Isn't the excitement in not knowing what the outcome will be? However, by using certain skills you can influence the outcome? That means the more understanding you have of the sales process the more you will be able to deal with the every day ups and downs you have in sales. This is also the reason why management gets frustrated with the sales department. Management wants an exact, predictable outcome, which is not possible unless the sales department is given the tools and training to improve the skills of the sales team and improve the outcome.

Here is how you can use scientific principles to increase your sales: Focus on the activities and not so much on the outcome. Make a decision to do something and do it. That is scientific.

The 13 skills learned in this book are scientific principles that will greatly improve (not predict 100%) your success in sales.

I have been teaching and applying these scientific principles for more than 20 years. I know for a fact that the successful sales people improve the outcome of their activities by being more skilled in these 13 areas.

Make the decision to improve your skills. That is something you CAN do with a predictable outcome. Your sales will increase, but exactly how much is unpredictable. Let's just hope it is enough to keep yourself, your management and your family happy. However, if you don't do anything to improve your skills I can predict the outcome with scientific certainty. You will be this year's biggest loser.

How to handle rejection

You are probably being asked to make more sales calls and you are having a problem. Here's why:

More calls will result in more rejection.

Before I give you my technique for handling rejection let me share with you a comment I received some time ago when I published the following information in a magazine article.

"I just read your article, Handling Rejection - Understand Why. Wow! I started my new business a couple of months ago. I refined my business plan, got leads, did a direct mailing, then I was frozen at the follow up call. I didn't have cold calling, or follow up call experience. Your article describes exactly how I feel and it has given me the confidence to act like I now have the right to place that call. Thank you for writing it. I really enjoyed it. And you probably made me lots of money because now I'm going to make my calls."

The reason the comment is so important is to let you know that you are not alone. Everybody in sales gets that FEELING. You know the one I'm talking about. If you don't it's only because you haven't been in sales long enough to make your first call. You are still under the delusion that everyone wants to see you and buy from you.

Here is the biggest reason you don't make the call in the first place:

You are worried about what they will think of you if you are unable to answer a tough question they might ask, or overcome an objection?

Here's a secret - they don't think about you.

Most people spend 98% of their time thinking about themselves. In the 2% of time left over there is not much room to squeeze you in.

It has always been amazing to me how some people can let negative thoughts or comments occupy so much space in their mind. Some people let these thoughts freeze their activities and kill their career in sales. Every thought you carry around and dwell on should be paying rent for taking up space in your mind!

I am always impressed with people who have conquered their fear of rejection. I am much more impressed with them then I am the people who happen to stumble onto a big sale. I am always looking for them because I am so eager to learn how they do it.

Here's an example and a good lesson in rejection.

My wife and I were in the kitchen and noticed two young gentlemen with white shirts and black ties approaching our front door. My wife told me to answer the door.

I really enjoy talking with people so I greeted the visitors eager to ask them some questions. The two young men were of a certain religious faith on a mission. During the conversation I asked them how many doors they had to knock on before someone invited them in. They said on a good day ONE OUT OF FIFTY will talk to us! Think of it - FORTY NINE PEOPLE TURNED THEM DOWN BEFORE ONE WOULD TALK TO THEM. I asked them how they handled the 49 who rejected them and here is what they told me: "We pray for them!"

Now there's a plan! Instead of letting them upset you why not just say to yourself: "That person has such a closed mind he won't even listen to me and with that kind of an attitude his business will probably go belly up because of his lack of interest in anything new! Since I don't see his name on the bail-out list I'd better send up a prayer for him because he is going to need more help then I can possibly give him anyway!!"

What just happened? YOU rejected HIM!

And THERE LIES THE KEY TO YOUR SUCCESS.

If your closing ratio for opening new customers is 1 out of every 10 here is what you have to do: Line up 10 calls with the idea that 9 will tell you to get lost! Nine of them are going to try to humiliate you. Nine of them are going to try and make you fail.

It's really a good thing for us in sales that there are a lot of dumb bunnies out there anyway.

Why?

Because they help the sales profession from becoming overcrowded. Let the other professions lock themselves in an office from 8 to 5 and quiver every time the boss walks by. Let the willy-nilly wimps take care of all those mundane activities. Let the timid non assertive people who wake up every day in fear of their job hope and pray there is someone out there who knows how to CREATE BUSINESS. WHO KNOWS THAT BEING REJECTED IS PART OF THE GAME.

It takes "GUTS" to be in sales.

I looked the word "guts" up in the thesaurus - here's what came back - courage, dauntlessness, heart, mettle, moxie, pluck, resolution, spirit, backbone, grit, intestinal fortitude, nerve, spunk! Put THAT list next to the phone or on the dash board because THAT DESCRIBES YOU!

When somebody rejects you just say this:

"Two words for you buddy - thank you!" You are simply that much closer to finding a REAL customer.

The bigger the stakes, the bigger the chance for rejection. If you were playing in the Super Bowl and your team lost because YOU fumbled the ball THAT would be the ultimate rejection. How many millions of people would be rejecting you? Without taking that risk of rejection you lose before you even start. You will never be in the Super Bowl of Sales.

Nobody likes rejection. It's natural to feel some disappointment when you hear someone say "no."

The issue is how you deal with that rejection. When you hear no it means you are doing your job.

The issue of rejection is not what the prospect or customer thinks of you, but what you think of yourself.

Another important part of dealing with rejection is understanding why they rejected you.

Here is what I mean.

The reason may have to do with timing - at this particular moment in time, as you are making your sales call, they may be perfectly happy with their current vendor. They may have just had a fight with their spouse and you happen to be the first one they talk to. They may have not had anything to eat all day and it is affecting their mood. They may have just been turned down for a promotion - or a loan - or a new job. They may have just had to fire one of their employees. All these things have nothing to do with you.

You have to train your mind to respond to rejection with enthusiasm.

I sold insurance many years ago and part of the training program was to go into a small office and make 10 cold phone calls. The phone was wired with speakers so the rest of the trainees could sit in the adjoining room and listen to the conversations. After you made your phone calls you would be critiqued by your colleagues. That was easy. The hard part is when you are by yourself sitting in your car waiting for your appointment time, or when you are sitting alone at your desk in your home office and have to make the call. THAT is when it strikes.

A friend told me about a company where he applied for a job. The company sold something OTHER than vacuum cleaners. They sold computers. Yet, as part of his job qualification program he had to sit in a room with a telephone and phone book, call 100 people at random and try to get an appointment to do a vacuum cleaner demonstration. Over half of the applicants would quit before they made it to 50 calls.

This fear of rejection could be costing you a lot of money if you are not making calls because of it.

How do you overcome this fear of approaching someone? Here's what you have to do even if you don't feel like it - you have to ask.

The bottom line of selling is to ask for your customer's or prospect's business. Don't be afraid to do just that. Don't be embarrassed to ask for what you want. Don't fear rejection. Don't worry about making the customer angry. Don't be immobilized by your own timidity. Don't have negative thoughts that will set you up for failure.

Instead say to yourself... "I love what I do - I love to sell. I am in the right place at the right time. I have nothing to lose and everything to gain by making the call and asking for the business."

Selling is really simple. Selling is asking enough people to buy your products and services. Selling is weeding out all the one's that don't "get it." All you have to do is ask enough people to buy your products and services and SOMEONE WILL BUY! If you don't make the request the customer is already ahead - you've made things easy for them! You've eliminated the possibility that they might actually say yes.

Don't let fear of rejection keep you from making the call. Approach each prospect with the idea that you are qualifying THEM. Do they qualify to buy from ME? Do they have the means to pay for what I'm selling? Are they smart enough to realize the value of what I am offering? Are they worth the investment of my valuable time? Is there enough business on the table for me to spend time and money to get my share?

When calling on a new prospect those are the questions you want answered. When you make a prospect call or a cold call, there is always a certain amount of hesitation because the pressure is on YOU to make a presentation. Forget about making a presentation. Go in with the attitude that you are QUALIFYING THEM. If they don't measure up THEY are the poor souls that miss out! They are the ones that lose.

Read this next sentence carefully. To reduce call hesitation when calling on a prospect, make the call with the idea that you are qualifying the prospect and you can reject THEM if they don't measure up. Now you have the power. You have the power of rejection. You don't like to be rejected. So why give anyone the power to reject you? You are simply making the call to INVESTIGATE.

You are there to get the FACTS ABOUT THEM. What you have to sell may be way beyond their understanding. It may be way over their head. To find out, you have to make the call and do the interview.

There is a certain fear you feel when trying to sell something to a stranger. But now you are not trying to sell on that initial contact. You are eliminating unqualified prospects. Don't let fear of rejection keep you from picking up the phone and making the call. You - your products - your services - are the answer to their prayers.

Are they good enough to do business with YOU!

A confident sales team

What is the key to keeping your sales team confident and motivated?

What is the key that will unlock the potential of your sales team and get them excited about reaching their potential? The answer is to take a new approach. The secret is to make the transition from having a group of independent contractors to a team of highly motivated sales professionals working for the success of the entire company. The key word is "team!"

Here's where you start.

Let's say you have 50 sales people and you are going to put together a sales contest to get them motivated. You have a first place, second place, and third place winner. If I am one of your sales team members what would I be thinking? "I already know who is going to win, they always win, so why put in the effort?" You end up with 3 winners and 47 losers! You have everyone working out of self interest rather than being a team player. You have everyone competing against each other.

You have a team of losers!

You have just reinforced the fact that the majority of your sales people are losers. To get your sales team motivated you have to do more than offer a simple contest, you have to offer a program. You have to reinforce the fact that every member of your team is a winner.

Your competition is not your own team members! Your competition is your competitor. The ones out there taking your business! It's true that fear of loss will get someone going in the short term, but what about for the long haul? Everybody reaches a point where they decide to "chuck it" if they don't feel like an important member of the team!

When I was in the military I was part of a team. There was never any question or doubt about it. If I made a mistake, we all suffered. If I did something outstanding, we were all rewarded. From the first day of boot camp until the day of final discharge, I was a team member. "I've got your back" was not just a cute little phrase; it meant that if I had to take a bullet for you, I would! Being a Veteran, I still feel like a member of the team.

Here's a case study to show you exactly what I mean.

An insurance company I did business with several years ago had just completed the best year they ever had in their history, doubling their sales for the year. I asked the VP of sales what the secret was.

First, he came up with a slogan for the year; "We Appreciate Every Member of Our Team of Agents". Then they set up a program to prove it. The entire support staff was told to go out of their way to make sure the agents in the field were taken care of and made to feel important. They put together an incentive trip that was all or nothing. If every agent made their numbers the entire company would go. If they didn't, no one would go.

They took it a couple of steps further. At the start of the year they sent flowers to all the agent's spouses and said they appreciate the long hours and evenings away from home (making their spouse feel like part of the team). During the year they sent monthly cards to their spouses showing the great trip they would be going on at the end of the year.

The sales that were required to win the trip were attainable and the entire "team" would be in a position to go. The program was so successful they broke every record in the industry.

Half way through the year they were actually helping each other rather than competing. Anyone who was running behind was given all the help and advice they needed to make their numbers. That's what you call a team effort.

It could have been a brand new sales person who landed a small account that made all the difference. One that actually took more work, more effort, more planning, more calls, more follow up and more rejection to land. He or she was motivated because they knew how important every sale was for the "team!" It could have been that small sale that put the final number on the score board and pushed them over the top. It's a valuable point for everybody and when it goes up on the score board, everybody wins!

It takes more than an individual effort to build a high level of confidence.

It takes the feeling that you are an important member of a team. An individual's motivation will double when they feel like an important member of a team. Build a team and you will find that everyone starts helping rather than competing. Build a team and it's easy to make individual decisions, because if it's good for the team, it's the right thing to do. If it's not, don't do it. Build a team and it's like the Marine creed of "no man left behind." Build a team and it takes on a life of its own. The team becomes more important than any single individual, yet all the individuals in the team benefit. Build a team and everyone feels more secure, resulting in more individual effort which equates to more sales. We are all on the same ship. If the ship sinks, we all go down!

Set the stage

Why do so many people come into selling and after a year or two they are gone? Why do sales people fail? Here are the reasons that sound good. These reasons justify, in the failures mind, the decision that selling is not for them. These reasons justify their failure.

"This is not worth it."
  "There must be a better way to make a living."
  "I'm going back to school and get a real job."
  "All the good territories are already taken."
  "The competition is ruthless."
  "I'm going to try selling a different line."
  "They expect too much."
  "How can they expect me to sell anything at these prices?"

The light at the end of the tunnel went out for these "would-be" sales people. They sold themselves on the idea that they were not "cut out to be in sales."

They saw only the glamour of being independent with opportunity to earn "easy" money. Do any of these reasons sound familiar? Yes- of course they do. We have all had these thoughts at some point.

So why does one person become an outstanding success at selling while another, with the same potential, fail?

You are parked behind a restaurant sitting in your car waiting for your appointment time. You could be selling them anything. Food, supplies, insurance, association membership. The person you are going to see is probably much older and more experienced than you. He is more than likely going to ask you something about your product line that you can't answer or don't know. As you are waiting, the anxiety grows. It is the middle of summer and the August sun is beating down on the pavement. As you get out of the car the heat and humidity are so thick you can cut it with a knife.

You walk past the dumpster and the smell practically makes you sick. As you open the door the heat from the kitchen hits you like a blast furnace. The person you are going to talk to is busy working. You know he sees you but he does not make eye contact with you. He is making you stand there as if you are invisible. At this moment in time the truth will reveal itself – are you, or are you not, going to succeed in a business with such a high failure rate? At this moment you will know how well you understand the principles and psychology of the buyer/seller relationship, or simply "The Principles of Selling."

If you DO NOT understand the PRINCIPLES your reaction is predictable. You get humiliated. Upset. Embarrassed. Mad. You take the prospects rudeness as a personal insult.

Your ego gets wounded and your mind starts filling up with negative thoughts. When he finally turns to talk to you, your attitude is reflected in your face. You try to get control of your attitude – but it's too late. The prospect won in the first round!

If you DO understand the PRINCIPLES your reaction is also predictable. You understand that you are a sales person and the prospect is on the defensive. They are afraid you are going talk them into something they do not want.

They are afraid you have a certain power over them and that is why they are ignoring you. By understanding the PRINCIPLES you know that the customer is simply setting the stage and sending you a message – a message that says he is important, his time is valuable, he is in control of this meeting. By understanding the PRINCIPLES you do not let the situation turn negative.

You say to yourself "I really love what I do – I love my profession."

"I really love playing the selling game."

"He's made his first move and he is doing it quite well."

"When he does acknowledge me I will greet him with a smile and attitude of appreciation."

Do you see the difference? So, what is the reason so many sales people fail?

The person who fails usually has been thoroughly trained in the products and services they are going to sell - they have NOT been trained in the psychology and principles of selling.

Sounds simple, I know.

Most non-selling managers and business owners believe that successful sales people are born that way. This is simply not true. A sales person needs professional training just as much as a doctor, lawyer, airline pilot, accountant, carpenter or chef. Why should selling be any different?

Successful sales people learn the principles of selling and apply them. Sales people who fail do not learn the principles of selling and rely on their ability to "wing it", which ultimately lets them down.

ATTITUDE MANAGEMENT.

Not just having a positive attitude – but managing your attitude under all the various selling situations. Programming your mind to react in a certain way in a specific situation. It does no good to read about something as important as attitude management and then do nothing about it.

To manage your attitude you must monitor your thoughts and feelings under every selling situation. Approach it as if you were doing a scientific study. When you find that you are reacting negatively to a specific situation, you have found an opportunity to sharpen your skill.

Which statements are true?

T F   It's part of a customer's job to ask for a discount.

Your customer will be on the defensive before you even begin to sell. "You're going to have to sharpen your pencil to do business with me." "That price is unacceptable." "You sure are proud of your products." Or other indications that they want a lower price. They won't get a better price if they don't ask. They have nothing to lose and everything to gain by asking you for a price reduction. Especially when everything is going up as fast as it is.

T F   A customer should ask for a discount at least twice.

Any customer whose attended a buying seminar has been taught to ask for price concessions at least TWICE before settling. By knowing what to expect you can be better prepared. How do you deal with price objections without giving in and losing your companies money and your commission?

T F   A customer wants you to believe price is most important.

You can usually expect a customer to ask about price before you even start talking about the benefits. A customer may not understand the difference between what you offer and what your competitors offer and focus on price first. They may misunderstand the costs and marketing assistance you offer. Most likely they're just looking for a better price. What do you say? Are you prepared for this BEFORE you make the call?

T F   You will always have competitors with lower prices.

There will be competitors who are cheaper! There will always be someone who's figured out how to deliver things a little cheaper than you can. There will always be a competitor who doesn't know their real costs and is willing to give away their gross profit by selling on nothing but price. How should you respond when the customer says your competitor's price is better? This is easy for them to say and difficult for you to respond. Try asking for specifics. Gain an advantage by asking, "In what way are they better?"

T F   Your confidence will influence your gross profit.

Your customer will believe the things about your company that you believe. The more confidence you have in your company the more confidence the customer will have in you. That is why confidence is so important.

You and I both know they are all true.

Here's the question: If it is a blow to your confidence every time you are presented with them there is only one conclusion. You need to be better prepared. You need to go into every meeting with solid product knowledge and reasons that help you approach the sale with more confidence.

Confidence: Remove restrictions and limitations

I am confident because I have removed the self imposed restrictions and limitations that hold people back from accomplishing all they can. My goal is to become a highly skilled sales professional. I have made a total commitment and it is reflected in every action I take and every task I perform. While my colleagues and competitors are always looking for an easier way to get their job done by reducing the amount of service they give, I am perfecting the skills that will make me a major league player in my own game, the game of selling. My confidence goes deep because I have earned it by attending sales meetings with enthusiasm, investing in time beyond my company training to improve my skills, and setting high goals.

My 4% improvement objective:

_____

_____

_____

_____

_____

_____

What the entire course will do for you

Buying all 13 books is like buying a library of 13 powerful coaching sessions that will increase every skill necessary for generating business. Once you experience the seemingly effortless improvement you will understand why there is a picture of Ben Franklin on every 100 dollar bill.

You will learn how to improve relationships, improve management skills, be more productive, generate more customers, negotiate better contracts, open new accounts, earn more profits and create more sales! Results most people only dream about! If you are a sales professional or an entrepreneur this is the perfect program to boost your sales and increase your profits.

Ben Franklin's system

In our fast paced business and personal life today it has become increasingly difficult to set aside time for self development and improving your skills. With every spare minute taken up by reading blogs, logging on to Facebook, following people on Twitter, responding to text messages and emails and constantly talking on your cell phone, there seems to be little, if any, time left for learning new skills. Even the quiet time behind the wheel of your car is no longer available with satellite radio and cell phone coverage in every corner of the country.

Even though this seems like a new problem, distractions have been around forever. Two hundred years ago a man by the name of Ben Franklin had the same problem. He concluded that it was not a matter of distractions as much as a matter of focus. He set out to solve the problem and created the most effective system for self improvement ever invented.

Ben Franklin gives credit for all his success and accomplishments to the implementation of this system for the success he sought after. Despite being born into a poor family and only receiving two years of formal schooling, Ben Franklin became a successful printer, scientist, musician, author and one of the founding fathers of the United States. Ben Franklin is considered to have been one of the most persuasive and successful people in the history of the United States. He was a very skilled sales person, marketer, negotiator and copywriter. Skills that every business owner, professional person, manager and marketer should have.

In the year 1723, Ben Franklin, at the age of seventeen, arrived in Philadelphia without a penny to his name. At age 42, he retired, wealthy, the first self made millionaire in the country. Few people, before or since have ever been as successful as Benjamin Franklin. He gave credit for his many inventions and business successes to his system for self improvement he created when he was 20 years old.

The key to Franklin's success was his drive to constantly improve himself and accomplish his ambitions. In order to accomplish his goal, Franklin developed and committed himself to a personal improvement program that consisted of mastering 13 principles.

When he was seventy-nine years old, Benjamin Franklin wrote more about this idea than anything else that ever happened to him in his entire life. He felt that he owed all his success and happiness to this one thing. Franklin wrote: "I hope, therefore, that some of my descendants may follow the example and reap the benefit."

Since success is developed by performing small and seemingly insignificant acts, you can use this method by reading and putting into practice the 13 skills that will guarantee your success in sales with scientific certainty.

This program takes advantage of Franklin's system and applies it to improving your skills as a sales professional. This program will show you how to dominate your market by first dominating yourself. By focusing on the 13 skills that make up a highly effective and successful sales professional. As these skills are improved your results and sales increases will also show a dramatic improvement.

The goal of going through the program the first time is to increase each skill by only four percent. With the accomplishment of this small improvement in each skill or attitude your overall improvement will be 52%. Those are results most people only dream about. However, you can accomplish this by investing as little as 45 minutes once a week reading one book and then focusing on improving the single skill during the rest of the week. The second week by reading the second book and focusing on that single skill during the week and so on until all 13 weeks are completed.

You can write the single word on the back of your business card and tape it to your dash board as a reminder. You can put this one word on your smart phone as a reminder as well as on your email signature, your Facebook page or you can even have something worthwhile to tweet about. One word, one week, one skill, one "I am" statement, 4% improvement objective and your subconscious mind will receive the message through all the clutter and act on it.

After the first time through the process you can do as Ben Franklin suggests and go through the program a second, third and fourth time. Get your whole sales team on the same page at the same time and you will experience a whirlwind of new excitement and new business. Or get a like minded colleague and join forces with accountability and focus.

1. Attitude Define what you want and go after it.
2. Respect Earn respect-no more comfort zone.
3. Service Help customers build their business.
4. Urgency Be enthusiastic get things done now.
5. Confidence Remove restrictions and limitations.
6. Persistence Keep going and never give up.
7. Planning Get big results by setting big goals.
8. Questions Ask questions that make the sale.
9. Attention Get attention with irresistible offers.
10. Presenting Give reasons why they should buy.
11. Objections Remove every roadblock to the sale.
12. Closing Ask for the order and get paid.
13. Follow up Remove all hope for competitors.

About the author Bob Oros (BobOros.com),

Bob Oros has been a full time speaker and author since 1992 with over 2,000 speaking engagements in all 50 states and several international locations as well as the author of 21 books on sales. Prior to starting his speaking career, Bob served six years in the US Navy as a Communications Specialist and then worked his way from a street sales person to the position of National Sales Manager for a Fortune 200 company.

CSP Award: Bob was awarded the designation of Certified Speaking Professional (CSP) by the National Speakers Association and the International Federation for Professional Speakers. Fewer than 10% of all speakers worldwide qualify for this award.

PWA Member: Bob is a member of the Professional Writers Alliance.

www.ingramcontent.com/pod-product-compliance
Lightning Source LLC
Chambersburg PA
CBHW072252170526
45158CB00003BA/1063